RODEOS

RODEOS

The Greatest Show on Dirt

by Judith Alter

A First Book

FRANKLIN WATTS
A DIVISION OF GROLIER PUBLISHING
New York   London   Hong Kong   Sydney
Danbury, Connecticut

Photographs ©: AP/Wide World Photos: 9; The Bettmann Archive: 13, 15, 16, 36, 38, 46, 57; Folio Inc.: cover, 11, 23, 26, 28, 29, 41, 55 (Jerry Wachter), 20, 25 (David Lissy), 33 (John A. Sawyer), 30-31 (Mark MacLaren); Gamma-Liaison: 44; Linda St. Dennis: 21; North Wind Picture Archives: 51; Superstock, Inc.: 52; UPI/Bettmann: 2, 39, 49.

Author photograph ©: Smiley's Studio

Library of Congress Cataloging–in–Publication Data

Alter, Judy, 1938–
    Rodeos : the greatest show on dirt / Judith Alter.
       p. cm.—(A First book)
    Includes bibliographical references (p.) and index.
    Summary: Presents a brief history of rodeos, descriptions of the various competitive events and their rules, and discussion of some of the legendary competitors, both men and women.
      ISBN 0-531-20245-3 (lib.bdg.)   ISBN 0-516-15816-0 (pbk.)
      1. Rodeos—United States—Juvenile literature. [1. Rodeos.]
I. Title. II. Series.
GV1834.A58 1996
791.8'2—dc20   96-12143
                                                       CIP
                                                        AC

CONTENTS

TALL IN THE SADDLE

Not yet thirty years old, Ty Murray of Stephenville, Texas, is already a rodeo legend. Murray was rodeo's all-around champion for six straight years. Cowboys and fans call him "The Million Dollar Kid," because his earnings reached $100,000 faster than those of anyone else in rodeo history. Riding in three **rough stock** events (saddle bronc riding, bareback bronc riding, and bull riding) at a 1993 rodeo, Murray set an earnings record of just under $125,000 for a single competition.

Murray is a member of the Professional Rodeo Cowboys Association (PRCA), along with over six thousand other professional rodeo competitors and about three thousand "permit-holders," or apprentice members. To qualify for membership, a cowboy must earn $2,500 as a permit-holder at PRCA events. From its headquarters in Colorado Springs, Colorado, the PRCA administers rodeo as a professional sport, setting contest rules and judging standards. It sanctions, or approves, close to one thousand rodeos across the nation each year, a large majority of them in the western United States.

The most prestigious rodeo for participants is the PRCA's National Finals Rodeo. In this rodeo, competition is open only to the top fifteen cowboys in each event. Prize money at the National Finals Rodeo is in the millions of dollars. It is at this rodeo that the PRCA names the year's all-around champion based on points earned throughout the year at recognized rodeos.

Six-time all-around rodeo champion Ty Murray stands in front of a Boeing 737, whose tail bears an image of him in action.

The PRCA is not the only rodeo association active today. Another, smaller organization is the International Professional Rodeo Association (IPRA), which sanctions about five hundred rodeos a year. The IPRA, founded in the 1950s in Oklahoma to organize the sport in the eastern states, holds its own national finals rodeo and names an all-around champion each year. This rodeo association is also known for being the first to recognize women's barrel racing as a championship event. There is also the Women's Professional Rodeo Association. It sanctions all-women events, holds a National Finals Rodeo for professional cowgirls, and names an all-around champion each year.

In addition, there are many amateur rodeo organizations. They include regional and minority as well as collegiate and high school associations.

Clearly, rodeo is big sport, big entertainment, and big business—but it wasn't always so.

Even young riders take part in rodeo competitions.

THE FIRST
RODEOS

Rodeo began as an informal contest between working cowboys in a small town in the American West. To break the boredom of cowboy life and to celebrate the end of a cattle roundup, the men competed against each other to test the skills they used every day: roping and tying steers and riding bucking horses. Which town hosted the first rodeo competition? Several claim the honor.

The first rodeos showcased the skills cowboys used in their daily work.

Some folks say the first contest was held on July 4, 1864, in Prescott, Arizona. Others say the competition held in the small town of Pecos in Texas on July 4, 1883, was in fact the first rodeo. That day, Tray Windham roped and tied a steer in twenty-two seconds, winning a prize of forty dollars. Still others claim the honor for Cheyenne, Wyoming; Miles City, Montana; Piney Ridge, Arkansas; San Angelo and Tascosa in Texas; and finally North Platte, Nebraska.

On July 4, 1882, William "Buffalo Bill" Cody staged his first Wild West show in his hometown of North Platte. The show, called "The Old Glory Blowout," was a combination of competitive events and frontier demonstrations. By the 1890s, Cody's show included dramatic reenactments of stagecoach robberies, Indian massacres, and buffalo hunts performed by hired hands. Before long, rodeos and Wild West shows were closely linked and remained so until the disappearance of the Wild West shows in the 1920s. Although some say rodeos began with Cody's show, Buffalo Bill cannot be credited with inventing rodeo.

Unlike Wild West shows, rodeos remained competitions between working cowboys. For many years, they were informal contests often staged on July 4. Cowboys who entered these rodeos hoped to win as much prize

An 1886 advertisement announces an appearance of Buffalo Bill and his troupe.

AT ERASTINA WOODS
Mariners' Harbor, Staten Island.
BOATS FROM THE BATTERY.   FARE 10 CENTS.

Buffalo Bill's

Wild West

A FLEET OF STEAMERS From all Local Points.
For Particulars See Daily Papers.

money as Tray Windham had in Pecos. However, these cowboys never considered quitting their day jobs to take up rodeoing as a profession.

Before long, there were traveling rodeos or bronc shows throughout the West. Cowboys usually walked the horses and cattle from town to town. There were no arenas or fairgrounds back then. Often a wide, roped-off street or an empty pasture had to do for a performance area. The cowboys' livelihoods depended on the size of the crowd the show drew. If a large number of people paid admission,

the cowboys ate well. If the crowd was thin, the cowboys ate cold biscuits.

By 1915, four rodeos offered two- and three-day money contests for cowboys. They were the California Rodeo in Salinas, Frontier Days in Cheyenne, Wyoming, the Calgary Stampede in Alberta, Canada, and the Oregon Round-Up in Pendleton. These classic rodeos, still in operation today, brought fame—and tourists—to their small hometowns.

In the 1920s, rodeo went east to the New York Stampede in Brooklyn and the great Madison Square Garden Rodeo in New York City. During these years, the nature of rodeo changed. Participants were no longer working cowboys showing off their skills. They were men who considered rodeo their calling and themselves as professional athletes.

Another big change came in 1936. A group of cowboys entered in a show at the Boston Garden went on strike for fairer distribution of prize money. They called themselves the Cowboy Turtle Association. The use of *turtle* in the group's name was a poke at themselves for

A rodeo participant gets thrown at one of the first Calgary Stampedes, an event held annually in Alberta, Canada.

being so slow to organize and improve what was by now a profession.

The Turtles went on to achieve better pay, fairer judging, and standardized events for themselves. The group became the Rodeo Cowboys Association (RCA) in 1945 and the Professional Rodeo Cowboys Association (PRCA) in 1975.

STANDARD RODEO EVENTS AND RULES

oday's rodeo performances consist of several standard events: saddle bronc riding, bareback bronc riding, bull riding, calf roping, and steer wrestling. There is also barrel racing, which is primarily a women's event. Each event has clearly defined standards by which it is judged.

Saddle bronc riding, bareback bronc riding, and bull riding are called rough stock events, because cowboys

A competitor in the saddle bronc riding event takes a turn in front of rodeo officials and fans.

ride rough, or untrained, animals. Calf roping and steer wrestling are the timed events where speed is crucial.

In the saddle and bareback bronc riding events, a cowboy tries to stay on an unbroken horse called a **bronc** for an eight-second ride. When the music stops and the buzzer indicates the end of the eight seconds, a mounted cowboy called a **pickup man** moves in. Riding close to the contestant, the pickup man will give him a hand so that he can slide off the rough animal to safety. There are usually two pickup men in the ring to do what they can for the safety of the cowboy.

Considered rodeo's classic event, saddle bronc riding requires the cowboy to show style as well as stamina on his ride on a saddled bronc. He is judged equally on how well he rides and how well the horse bucks. Riders draw horses randomly. A horse lacking in spirit will not win many points for the rider. A horse that bucks and **sunfishes** will win more points for the cowboy.

The more a bronc bucks, the more points a cowboy wins, as long as he stays mounted.

For his part, the rider is judged by his **spurring**. Spurring is the raking of the animal's shoulders with metal spurs, which attach to the rider's heel, to urge the animal to buck. More points are awarded for long, smooth spur strokes extending from the horse's neck to the saddle. Spur strokes must be in rhythm with the horse's jumping. The cowboy's feet should be straight out in front when the bronc's feet hit the ground. The cowboy's feet should strike the back of the saddle, with his knees bent, when the horse lunges into the air.

The eight-second ride is scored on a scale of one hundred. There are fifty possible points for how the horse bucks and fifty for how the rider spurs and with how much style. A score in the sixties is considered good; one in the seventies is excellent.

Bareback bronc riding grew out of rodeo rather than ranch life. In fact, working cowboys rarely attempted to ride a wild horse bareback. Today, this event provides some of the wildest action in rodeo.

As in saddle bronc riding, in bareback riding, a rider must stay on for eight seconds and is judged on his spurring. The cowboy uses a leather rigging held on the horse's back by a cinch and an attached strap that he wraps around his hand. One dread of cowboys and audiences alike is that a pitched cowboy won't get his hand

A wildly bucking bronc and an experienced cowboy make the bare- back riding event a real crowd-pleaser.

loose in time to escape being dragged like a helpless puppet. Bareback riding, it is said, is much like riding a jackhammer with one hand. Bareback riders say that it is not as easy as that.

The most dangerous and thrilling of rodeo events is bull riding, introduced to the rodeo world in the 1920s. It is usually saved for the final act of a performance. With only spurs, a riding glove, and a flat braided hemp rope with a woven handhold, the rider must stay eight seconds on an animal that weighs more than 1 ton (907 kg) and is as quick as he is big.

In bull riding, the cowboy places one gloved hand in the handhold and pulls the rope tightly around the bull, holding the end of the rope in his hand. He will be disqualified for touching the animal or himself with his free hand, using sharp spurs, or placing spurs under the rope as it is being tightened. Spurring is not required but will earn extra points. A bull that twists and spins in addition to bucking will receive an even better score.

During the ride, the cowboy is in danger of losing his balance and allowing the bull's horns to hit him. The greatest danger, however, comes when he dismounts the bull. Unlike horses, bulls have a tendency to attack the rider after he jumps off.

Bull riding is by far rodeo's most dangerous event.

In bull riding, **rodeo clowns** are responsible for the rider's safety. Bullfighting clowns will distract the bull long enough for the rider to get away. They also free the occasional contestant thrown from a bull with his hand caught in the rigging. Rodeo clowns resemble circus clowns. They have painted faces and wear raggedy clothes—baggy, cut-off jeans, a Hawaiian shirt, and a cowboy hat. But these clowns are deadly serious about the dangerous work they do.

A rodeo clown takes a short break from his work in the arena.

In recent years, new competitions have sprung up for rodeo clowns that demonstrate their bull-fighting skills. These contests have little to do with traditional Spanish bull-fighting. Instead of a lance and a cape, these bullfighters compete with running shoes and padded barrels. (And, also unlike the outcome in Spanish bullfights, both man and bull leave the arena unharmed.) The competing clown must spend forty seconds in the arena with the bull. After the first buzzer, the bullfighting clown can choose to stay another thirty seconds. He is judged on how well he controls the action in the arena and how successfully he takes risks.

Calf roping, like saddle bronc riding, dates back to rodeo's early days and actual work on a ranch. Today's working cowboys still practice the useful skill of roping and tying calves.

A race against the clock, calf roping requires teamwork between the cowboy and his horse. The luck of the draw also plays a part. In contrast to the rough stock events, a lively animal is not preferred in calf roping. A calf that runs fast or kicks hard can slow a cowboy's time.

In the calf roping event, the calf is released from a chute while the rider waits behind a barrier. If the cowboy breaks the barrier before the calf is released, he is penalized ten seconds. After the calf's head start, the cowboy chases the animal on horseback.

A good horse will then close in on the calf quickly and keep a steady distance between them, giving the cowboy his best chance to catch the calf with his **lariat**. The horse is trained to stop when the calf is roped and to keep the rope taut so that the calf cannot escape. At the same time, the cowboy dismounts, runs down the rope, and **flanks**—throws by hand—the calf to the ground.

Throughout the action, the cowboy has carried in his teeth a short rope called a pigging string. He uses this string to tie three of the calf's legs together. The clock is stopped when the cowboy throws his hands in the air, signaling that the calf is tied. However, the calf must remain tied for six seconds after the cowboy remounts his horse.

Holding a pigging string in his mouth and a lariat in his hand, a roper closes in on the calf.

Six to seven seconds in the calf roping event is a great time; ten seconds is "pretty good." As a calf roping entrant once said, "The difference between winning and losing can be just fractions of a second."

Steer wrestling, also called bulldogging, was introduced in a Wild West show by an African-American cowboy named Bill Pickett. It soon became a regular rodeo event. The event's name comes from the mixed-breed dogs cowboys called bulldogs. These dogs would nip at the heels of a steer and bark to make the animal charge. Once the steer was in the clear, away from the other cattle, the dog would jump up and sink its teeth into the steer's tender nose, and the steer would try to shake the dog loose. The weight of the dog would bring the steer down with a thud, and the cowboy could then rope the animal for branding or doctoring.

In calf roping, cowboys have only seconds to tie up any three of the calf's legs.

Steer wrestling is an event that requires two men. One is the **hazer**, who keeps the steer running straight. The other is the **dogger**, who makes the catch.

As in calf roping, in steer wrestling, the animal is given a head start. The dogger then rides after the steer, keeping his horse on the left side of the animal, while the hazer rides on the right. As the pair of cowboys ride alongside the steer, the dogger slides off his horse and onto the steer, his arms around its horns and his boot heels digging into the ground. He then wrestles the animal to the ground.

In steer wrestling, the dogger tries to wrestle the steer to the ground while the hazer keeps the steer moving in a straight line.

One rule is that the steer be on its feet before the cowboy topples it. The steer's head and all four legs must also be facing the same direction or the fall is illegal. If the fall is illegal, the steer is allowed to regain its feet and the cowboy can start all over again. Too many seconds are lost, however, to make that option worthwhile in competition.

Team roping is a third timed event sometimes found in rodeo. In this event, two contestants—a **header** and a **heeler**—work together to earn one time. A steer is released from the chutes with a slight head start, as in steer wrestling. This time, however, the header throws his rope over the steer's head or horns and wraps, or **dallies**, it to the saddle horn. As the rope becomes tight, the steer turns to the left, and the heeler catches the hind legs in a second loop and dallies it to his saddle horn. The clock is stopped when both horses are facing the steer and both ropes are taut.

In both rough stock and timed events, treatment of animals has been an issue almost since the first rodeo. Protests from animal rights activists in recent years have brought some changes to the arena, such as the "no-jerk-down" rule in calf roping. This means a **roper** loses points if the rope is taut and the calf is jerked off its feet.

Protests have also been lodged against the **flank straps** used on rough stock to increase an animal's buck-

In team roping, after the header ropes
the steer's head or horns, the heeler ropes
the animal's hind legs.

ing. Flank straps, however, have been proven not to harm the animals. Most horses and bulls stop bucking when the weight of a rider is gone, though the flank strap remains.

By and large, rodeo animals are well treated and cared for. They receive regular veterinary care, including vaccinations, and exercise. Stock contractors and rodeo officials claim that the animals, particularly rough stock, perk up when performance time comes, like an athlete who feels a rush of anticipation. One livestock veterinarian points out that it is only good business to take good care of the animals, since they provide the livelihood for the rodeo.

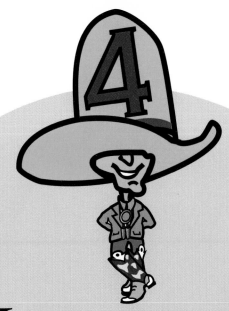

LEGENDARY COWBOYS

O ver the years, rodeo has produced some legendary competitors whose names live in cowboy lore and verse as well as rodeo records.

Bill Pickett, the man who introduced bulldogging, was one of the earliest rodeo legends. Born in Texas in 1860, Pickett gained fame when he rode with the Miller Brothers 101 Ranch Real Wild West show. According to Colonel Miller, owner of the Oklahoma-based show,

A group of cowboys pose in the rodeo ring.

Pickett "slid off a horse, hooked a steer with both hands on the horns, twisted its neck and then sank his teeth in the steer's nostrils to bring him down." Pickett claimed he first practiced the trick as a cowboy in South Texas, where the brush was too thick to use a lariat. Pickett died in 1932 at the age of seventy-two from injuries received while roping a bronc on the Miller 101 Ranch.

One of the most respected rodeo cowboys was Freckles Brown, a cowboy who continued to ride broncs and bulls well into his fifties, far past the age when most rodeo cowboys hang up their spurs. As a youngster, Brown rode broncs for fun at picnics in his home state of Wyoming. When he was sixteen, he rode his first bull. In 1967, at the National Finals Rodeo, he made rodeo history at the age of forty-six by riding a bull that had thrown all the other competitors. Brown also ranched in Oklahoma and ran a bullriding school for boys who wanted to follow in his rodeo steps but lacked the opportunity to learn the skills from real ranch work.

Casey Tibbs is another legendary name in rodeo history. Tibbs won six saddle bronc riding championships, a single bareback riding crown, and two all-around champion cowboy titles. One of ten children born in a South Dakota log house, Tibbs started rodeoing in the early 1940s at the age of fourteen. During his long career, he did rodeo acts, acted in the movies, was featured on the cover of *Life* magazine, collected rodeo stock, rode on trail drives, endorsed western clothes, and rode in old-timers' rodeos. Some called him the best-known rodeo cowboy ever.

Jim Shoulders, who rode rough stock in the 1950s, has won more championships than anyone else in the history of rodeo. He won four all-around championships, seven world titles in bull riding, and four in bareback riding in just eleven years. During his career, Shoulders saw rodeo recognized as a professional sport and was even featured in *Sports Illustrated*'s first-ever article about the rodeo. When he retired from the arena, Shoulders became a rodeo producer, owned rough stock, appeared in national advertising, conducted rodeo schools, and made documentary movies.

Casey Tibbs, shown here during competition, was one of a new breed of professional cowboys.

Jim Shoulders battles to stay on a bronc in the 1961 National Finals Rodeo.

Larry Mahan followed Shoulders in the 1960s, piling up championships and prize money riding bareback, saddle broncs, and bulls. He went on to run rodeo schools, have his own brand of Western clothes, and even author a handbook of rodeo riding. He was one of the first rodeo cowboys to retire wealthy.

Roy Cooper followed in rodeo history. By 1993, he had reached the National Finals Rodeo four times and earned several world titles—as well as over a million dollars—in calf and steer roping. Sometimes called "the Super Looper," Cooper began roping before he was ten. A natural athlete, he is known for his ability to concentrate under pressure and succeed at things that have never been done. Cooper has had surgery on both wrists and his back. Many thought his injuries would rule Cooper out of competition, but he has made remarkable comebacks.

And then there's today's legend, Ty Murray. Murray is one of the few cowboys who rides all three rough stock events. He says riding in all three makes him a better rider. Did success shock him? Not at all. Murray points out that rodeo success is not sudden; it grows out of years of preparation, riding day in and day out, traveling in sleet and mud and rain, going without sleep. "When you win it, you've worked for every inch of it," he once said.

Even with years of experience and hard work, rodeo competition is extremely dangerous, a fact Ty Murray learned firsthand in 1989. Murray was in the rodeo ring as a pickup man in Cheyenne, Wyoming, when his friend,

What makes rodeo one of the most exciting spectator sports also makes it one of the most dangerous.

twenty-five-year-old Lane Frost, rode a bull called Bad to the Bone. Frost made an eighty-five-point ride, but after he dismounted, the bull attacked him, killing him before Murray's eyes. A movie, *8 Seconds*, has been made of Frost's life.

WOMEN
IN RODEO

In most of today's rodeos, women ride in only one event—the barrel race, which many men refuse to ride in. Although rodeo has traditionally been a men's sport, the colorful history of women in rodeo began with the early days of the Wild West shows.

Women started riding in rodeos before the turn of the century. Annie Shaffer of Arkansas rode a bucking horse at Fort Smith in 1896. The next year, Bertha Kaepernick

Rodeos past and present have featured skilled horsewomen.

entered the wild horse race and rode broncs at Cheyenne's Frontier Days. The annual celebration was nearly drowned in a torrential rain, and the cowboys didn't want to ride in the mud. Kaepernick's brother persuaded her to do a demonstration ride to keep the audience from leaving and demanding their money back. Shamed by the woman rider, the cowboys went on to ride.

In 1901 when Prairie Rose Henderson, a rancher's daughter, tried to enter the contest in Cheyenne, the judges told her no women were allowed. She read the rules, pointed out that women were not mentioned, and got her ride.

By the early 1900s, women were competing in several rodeo events in Wild West shows. They rode in relay races, performed in dramatic episodes, and did trick riding. They sometimes rode in events many men shunned as too dangerous, like Roman races, where contestants rode standing on two horses, with a foot on each horse. They also did Pony Express races, which were mounted relays run by one rider on several horses. When it was time to change horses, the rider either went over the top of the saddle from one horse to the other without ever touching ground or vaulted to the ground with one step and sprang up onto the back of the next horse. Either way, it was dangerous.

Women also rode the rough stock in the early rodeos. Some rode with hobbled stirrups, which are stirrups tied together with a strap under the belly of the horse to make it easier to stay on the horse. Other women were afraid of getting their feet caught if they lost control of their ride and refused to ride with hobbled stirrups.

Over time, women were edged out of riding broncs.

Some men claim it was for their own protection after a few cowgirls were badly hurt and at least one killed, but some women have a different view. They say that when the Turtles organized and demanded more money, rodeo producers had to cut back and so cut out the smaller rough horses that the women rode.

One of the first cow-girls, who is often overlooked, is Lucille Mulhall of Oklahoma. Mulhall's father, Colonel Zack Mulhall, made a hand of his daughter at an early age and gave her a small herd of cattle when she was ten.

A cowgirl shows off superior horsemanship in a Wild West show.

st show, starring his
he roped a wolf in a
evelt, the vice presi-
girl," bringing national

stock and trick horses,
per. She is famous for
and performing such
riding abreast. She won
st everywhere she went.
ed vest from the Apache
the Queen of the Range,"
lded diamond and a rop-

ing scene set in on.

Lucille Mulhall was followed by Florence Randolph, a rider who was carried out for dead several times. In 1923, after a horse named School Girl somersaulted over on her and Randolph was pronounced dead in the arena, she made a miraculous recovery. Another time, after a bucking horse fell on her and she was told she would never walk again, Randolph jumped out of bed and rushed past the alarmed doctors into the night.

Fox Hastings was another woman active in rodeos during the 1920s. Once, when Hastings was thrown, the horse landed on her, tried twice to get up, and twice fell back on Hastings, who lay tangled in the rigging with her neck twisted. When she was finally carried from the ring, the crowd was sure she was dead. After fifteen minutes, Fox Hastings rode back into the arena in an open car and demanded a second ride. She rode splendidly, and few knew that she collapsed within minutes of dismounting from that second ride.

And then there was Tad Lucas who began her career—and her international reputation—in 1924 with a trip to England with a rodeo troupe. The youngest of twenty-four children, Lucas was born in Oklahoma and grew up as ranch children do—riding bareback and doing ranch chores. As a teenager, she rode wild stock that area ranchers brought to town every Saturday. The horses were **eared down**, or held by the ears, until the rider could mount. If the show was good, the crowd that had gathered to watch usually passed the hat to take up a contribution for the rider.

Tad Lucas was primarily a trick rider, though she did not learn trick riding until just before the first time she entered the rodeo arena. Her ranch background had given her the balance, timing, and coordination needed for her new calling. In 1925, Lucas was the all-around champion in Chicago and was later trick riding champion at Madison Square Garden for eight consecutive years. In 1940,

Fox Hastings falls from a horse during competition. Fortunately, her injuries were minor.

she won the Australian Trophy as best bronc rider at a competition in Sydney. Tad Lucas raised her daughter Mitzi in the arena and was still riding broncs in her fifties. Lucas gave up trick riding, she said, only when her horse got too old.

Today, women rarely ride rough stock or rope in all-around rodeos unless they are all-women shows. In PRCA rodeos, women ride the barrel race, which is a timed event.

In barrel racing, contestants must ride a 160-yard (146-m) cloverleaf pattern around three 55-gallon (210-l) drums, circling each drum on the way. For the sake of speed, riders make as tight a turn as possible around each barrel without knocking it over. Knocking over a barrel costs a five-second penalty. Then they urge their horses even faster on the exit. Today, timing is electronically done, and barrel racers can win by hundredths of a second.

The Women's Professional Rodeo Association sanctions events for women, including about a dozen all-women rodeos across the West. Standard events in these rodeos are bareback bronc riding, bull riding, team roping, and two kinds of calf roping—tie-down and breakaway, an all-women event.

In breakaway roping, instead of tying the calf down as they do in tie-down roping, the rider must simply lasso

Barrel racers must run their horses through the course as fast as possible without knocking over any of the three barrels.

the animal and bring her horse to a stop. The rope is tied to the saddle horn by a string or ribbon and, as the calf keeps running, it breaks the tie and pulls the rope from the horn.

Rough stock events for women are also modified. During the ride, which lasts six seconds instead of eight, the rider holds on to the rigging with one or two hands. She must indicate her choice before the animal leaves the chute.

A roper speeds past the crowd in pursuit of the calf.

Although roping is the fastest-growing part of women's rodeo, many feel that it is the rough stock events that bring in the crowds. Prize money for women is significantly less than that for men. Most female rodeo riders hold more traditional jobs while rodeoing for the love of it.

And just as Ty Murray is the wonder of men's rodeo, women's rodeo has a heroine today: she is barrel racer Charmayne Rodman. Rodman has won ten world championships in a row—more than any man in any event. She won the first when she was fourteen years old.

BACK TO THE BEGINNINGS

Today's rodeo is indeed big business. The sport has come a long way since the first traveling rodeos set up makeshift performance areas and hoped the crowds would come. These days the largest rodeo, the Houston Livestock Show and Rodeo, draws almost a million spectators every March.

Rodeo has become a professional competition between trained athletes. Rodeoing may not pay as well as some sports, like basketball or tennis, but the life is similar. Every action is dictated by the sport and almost every minute is spent practicing to be the best. Serious rodeo competitors also travel over 1,000 miles (1,609 km) a year to compete in over one hundred rodeos. The prize

Professional rodeo competitions require tremendous physical effort and practice.

money is better than it has ever been, but the danger is still the same. An old saying contends that it is not a question of if a rodeo cowboy will get hurt; it is just a question of when.

Producing a rodeo is no simple matter, and the behind-the-scenes people greatly outnumber the contestants. A rodeo begins with a producer, who coordinates all parts of the show. The producer is often a former contestant, and he is just as likely to also be the stock contractor—the person who provides healthy, lively animals for all events.

Then there are the pickup men, the specialty acts such as trick riders and animal acts that serve as a kind of half-time entertainment, officials and judges, secretaries and timers, an announcer with a dramatic voice and a good knowledge of rodeo, and a band to play, among other times, during each contestant's eight-second ride. There are people who act like stagehands, moving chutes into place, setting up barrels, and cleaning the arena when necessary. It takes a small army to put on a rodeo that meets the industry's strict standards for arena facilities, insurance, financial responsibility, and number and quality of livestock.

Some think that rodeos today have gotten too professional. With nostalgia for the past, they yearn for the

One thing that hasn't changed in the world of rodeo is competitor and spectator devotion to the sport.

informal rivalries that featured real ranch work. In the 1980s, team contests, called ranch competitions, were begun. The first, held at Wichita Falls, Texas, was called the Texas Ranch Roundup and featured cowboys and cowgirls from several area ranches. They competed in real-work events like branding and penning cattle and wild-cow milking. They earned more fun than money, but it was an old-time rodeo and a far cry from the commercialism of today's major rodeos. Perhaps someday rodeo will come full circle back to its beginnings.

Rodeo Terms

bronc — an unbroken horse chosen for its tendency to throw its rider

dally — to wrap a rope around a saddle horn

dogger — the cowboy who wrestles the steer to the ground in the steer wrestling, or bulldogging, event

ear down — to hold a horse by the ears until a rider mounts it

flank — to throw by hand

flank straps — the tight bands around an animal's hindquarters that are meant to increase its bucking

hazer — the mounted cowboy who keeps the steer running straight so that the second mounted cowboy can jump onto the steer in the steer wrestling, or bull-dogging, event

header — the cowboy who throws his rope over the steer's head or horns and wraps it to his saddle horn in the team roping event

heeler—the cowboy who catches the steer's hind legs in a loop and wraps it to his saddle horn in the team roping event

lariat—a lasso, or long rope with a noose, used to catch livestock

pickup man—a mounted cowboy who helps protect the contestant from the unbroken horse in the rodeo ring

rodeo clown—a bullfighter who protects the cowboy by distracting the bull when the rider dismounts or is thrown during the bull riding event

roper—a contestant in a roping event

rough stock—unbroken and untrained animals used in rodeo events

spurring—raking the animal's shoulders with metal spurs to urge it to buck

sunfish—to twist like a fish as a bronc does

FOR FURTHER READING

Acton, Avis. *Behind the Chutes at Cheyenne Frontier Days: Your Pocket Guide to Rodeo.* Cheyenne, Wyo.: ABC Publishing, 1991.

Bryant, Thomas A. *Rodeo: America's Number One Sport.* Basin, Wyo.: Wolverine Galley, 1986.

Coombs, Charles. *Let's Rodeo!* New York: Henry Holt, 1986.

Davidson, Mary R. *Buffalo Bill: Wild West Showman.* New York: Chelsea House, 1993.

Freedman, Russell. *Cowboys of the Wild West.* Boston: Houghton Mifflin, 1990.

Tomb, Ubet. *Cowgirls.* Santa Barbara, Calif.: Bellerophon, 1992.

INDEX

Page numbers in *italics* indicate illustrations.

About the Author

Judy Alter is the author of several dozen books for children, including *The Comanches* and *Women of the Old West* for Franklin Watts. She is the director of Texas Christian University Press, which publishes literature and history of Texas and the American West. Ms. Alter lives in Fort Worth, Texas.